MARX

Terry Eagleton

D0209285

ROUTLEDGE
New York

Published in 1999 by
Routledge
29 West 35th Street
New York, NY 10001

First published in 1997 by
Phoenix
A Division of the Orion Publishing Group Ltd.
Orion House
5 Upper Saint Martin's Lane
London WC2H 9EA

10 9 8 7 6 5 4 3 2 1

Library of Congress Cataloging-in-Publication Data

Eagleton, Terry, 1943–
      Marx / Terry Eagleton.
       p. cm.—(The great philosophers : 2)
      Includes bibliographical references.
      ISBN 0-415-92377-8 (pbk.)
      1. Marx, Karl, 1818–1883. I. Title. II. Series:
      Great Philosophers (Routledge (Firm)) : 2.
B3305.M74E24 1999
335.4'092—dc21
                                  99-24218
                                     CIP

To Steve Regan

MARX

and Freedom

PHILOSOPHY

Hegel and Aristotle were certainly philosophers, but in what sense was Karl Marx? Marx wrote a good deal that has a philosophical look about it; but he was also brusquely scornful of the philosophic mind, and declared in his celebrated eleventh thesis on Feuerbach that 'the philosophers have only interpreted the world, in various ways; the point, however, is to change it'.[1] One might riposte that it would be hard to change a world which we did not understand, were it not for the fact that Marx himself would surely agree. He is not out to replace ideas with mindless action, but to fashion a kind of practical philosophy which will help to transform what it is seeking to comprehend. Social and intellectual change go together: 'Philosophy cannot realize itself without the transcendence of the proletariat', he writes, 'and the proletariat cannot realize itself without the realization of philosophy.'[2] His second thesis on Feuerbach runs:

> The question whether objective truth can be attributed to human thinking is not a question of theory, but a *practical* question. In practice man must prove the truth, that is, the reality and power, the this-sidedness of his thinking. The dispute over the reality or non-reality of thinking which is isolated from practice is a purely *scholastic* question.[3]

This special kind of action-orientated theory is some-

3

times known as 'emancipatory knowledge', and has a number of distinctive features. It is the kind of understanding of one's situation that a group or individual needs in order to change that situation; and it is thus among other things a new *self*-understanding. But to know yourself in a new way is to alter yourself in that very act; so we have here a peculiar form of cognition in which the act of knowing alters what it contemplates. In trying to understand myself and my condition, I can never remain quite identical with myself, since the self which is doing the understanding, as well as the self understood, are now different from what they were before. And if I wanted to understand all *this*, then just the same process would set in. It is rather like trying to jump on one's own shadow or yank oneself up by one's hair. And since such knowledge also moves people to change their condition in a practical way, it becomes itself a kind of social or political force, part of the material situation it examines rather than a mere 'reflection' of or upon it. It is knowledge as an historical event rather than as abstract speculation, in which knowing *that* is no longer clearly separable from knowing *how*. Moreover, to seek to emancipate yourself involves questions of value, while knowing about your situation is a matter of factual comprehension; so here the usual distinction philosophy acknowledges between facts and values becomes interestingly blurred. It is not just that this kind of knowledge can be put to valuable use, but that the motivation for understanding in the first place is bound up with a sense of value.

The eleventh thesis on Feuerbach, then, is not just some sort of philistine appeal to turn from abstract speculation to the 'real world', though there was a streak of this brisk anti-intellectualism in the early Marx. Such an appeal forgets that without abstract concepts there would be no real world for us in the first place. The irony of Marx's gesture is that he makes this demand as a philosopher, not just as a political activist. He can thus be said to join a distinguished lineage of 'anti-philosophers', one which includes Kierkegaard, Nietzsche, Heidegger, Adorno, Benjamin, Wittgenstein, and in our own time such thinkers as Jacques Derrida and Richard Rorty, for whom there is something fundamentally awry with the whole philosophical enterprise of their time. For these men, philosophy itself, not just this or that topic within it, has become a deeply problematic pursuit. They therefore want either to transcend the whole project for reasons which remain *philosophically* interesting, or to find some way of recasting it in a new key entirely, an aim which for many of these thinkers means forging a new style of theoretical writing. Most of them are out to deflate the metaphysical pretentions of philosophy, outflanking them with something apparently more fundamental: being, power, difference, practical forms of life, or in Marx's case 'historical conditions'. An anti-philosopher of this kind differs from a mere opponent of philosophy in much the same way that an 'anti-novel' like *Ulysses* differs from a non-novel like the telephone directory.

Why was Marx so sceptical of philosophy? For one thing, he saw it as starting from the wrong place. Philosophy did not begin far back enough. The fashionable German philosophy of his day – Idealism – began from ideas, seeing consciousness as the foundation of reality; but Marx was aware that just for us to have an idea, a good deal else must already have taken place. What must already have happened in order for us to begin to reflect? We must already be practically bound up with the world we are pondering, and so already inserted into a whole set of relations, material conditions, social institutions:

> The production of ideas, of conceptions, of consciousness, is at first directly interwoven with the material activity and the material intercourse of men, the language of real life. Conceiving, thinking, the mental intercourse of men, appear at this stage as the direct efflux of their material behaviour. The same applies to mental production as expressed in the language of politics, laws, morality, religion, metaphysics, etc. of a people. Men are the producers of their conceptions, ideas, etc. – real, active men, as they are conditioned by a definite development of their productive forces and of the intercourse corresponding to these, up to its furthest forms. Consciousness can never be anything else than conscious existence, and the existence of men is their actual life-process.[4]

We should note here that while Marx wants, epistemologically speaking, to bind consciousness and the material world closely together, there is a *political* sense in which he wants to loosen up that relation. For him, as we shall see, we are most human and least like the other animals when we produce freely, gratuitously, independent of any immediate material need. Freedom for Marx is a kind of creative superabundance over what is materially essential, that which overflows the measure and becomes its own yardstick. It is just that, for all this to happen in society, certain material conditions are first required; so that the very 'excess' of consciousness over nature which Marx regards as a hallmark of our humanity is itself, ironically, a materially conditioned state of affairs. Where consciousness and social practice converge most obviously for Marx is in language itself:

> Language is as old as consciousness, language *is* practical, real consciousness that exists for other men as well, and only therefore does it also exist for me; language, like consciousness, only arises from the need, the necessity, of intercourse with other men. (GI 51)

But if language arises from need, as a necessary dimension of collective labour, it does not remain leashed to that necessity, as the phenomenon known as literature bears witness.

When it comes not just to 'consciousness', but to the systematic sort of reflection known as philosophy, then this clearly requires specialists, academies and a host of allied institutions, all of which can ultimately be funded only by the labour of others. This is one aspect of what Marx means by the division of mental and manual labour. Only when a society has achieved a certain economic surplus over material necessity, releasing a minority of its members from the demands of productive labour into the privilege of becoming full-time politicians, academics, cultural producers and so on, can philosophy in its fullest sense flower into being. Now thought can begin to fantasize that it is independent of material reality, just because there is a material sense in which it actually is:

Division of labour only becomes truly such from the moment when a division of mental and manual labour appears. (The first form of ideologists, *priests*, is concurrent.) From this moment onwards consciousness *can* really flatter itself that it is something other than consciousness of existing practice, that it *really* represents something without representing something real; from now on consciousness is in a position to emancipate itself from the world and to proceed to the formation of 'pure' theory, theology, philosophy, ethics, etc. (GI 51)

For Marx, culture really has only one parent, and that is labour – which for him is equivalent to saying, exploitation. The culture of class society tends to repress this unwelcome truth; it prefers to dream up for itself a nobler progenitor, denying its lowly parenthood and imagining that it sprang simply from previous culture, or from the unfettered individual imagination. But Marx is out to remind us that our thought, like our very physical senses, is itself a product of the history with which it engages. History – the real world – always in some way outruns the thought which seeks to enfold it, and Marx, who as a good dialectician emphasizes the dynamic, open-ended, interactive nature of things, detested those overweening systems of thought which (like Hegelian Idealism) believed that they could somehow stitch up the whole world within their concepts. It is darkly ironic that his own work would, among other things, give birth in time to just such sterile system-building.

The issue for Marx, then, is one of the material causes and

conditions of thought itself. We can inspect the causes of this or that, but can that thought round upon itself, so to speak, to grasp something of the history which produced it? Maybe for us moderns there are good reasons why this can never be wholly attained, why there is always some kind of blind spot, some necessary amnesia or self-opaqueness, which ensures that the mind will always ultimately fail in this endeavour. Marx himself, as a child of the Enlightenment, was perhaps rather more confident than we are in the translucent power of reason; but as an historicist thinker – and these twin currents, rationalist and historicist, are often in tension in his work – he recognized that if all thought was historical, then this must naturally be true of his own. There could not have been any Marxism in the age of Charlemagne or Chaucer, since Marxism is more than just a set of bright ideas which anyone, at any time, might have thought up. It is rather a time- and place-bound phenomenon, which acknowledges that the very categories in which it thinks – abstract labour, the commodity, the freely mobile individual and so on – could only have emerged from a heritage of capitalism and political liberalism. Marxism as a discourse emerges when it is both possible and necessary for it to do so, as the 'immanent critique' of capitalism, and so as a product of the very epoch it desires to move beyond. The *Communist Manifesto* is prodigal in its praise of the great revolutionary middle class, and of that mighty unshackling of human potential which we know as capitalism:

> The bourgeoisie, wherever it has got the upper hand, has put an end to all feudal, patriarchal, idyllic relations.

It has pitilessly torn asunder the motley feudal ties that bound man to his 'natural superiors', and has left remaining no other nexus between man and man than naked self-interest, than callous 'cash payment'. It has drowned the most heavenly ecstasies of religious fervour, of chivalrous enthusiasm, of philistine sentimentalism, in the icy water of egotistical calculation ... In one word, for exploitation, veiled by religious and political illusions, it has substituted naked, shameless, direct, brutal exploitation ... [It] has torn away from the family its sentimental veil, and has reduced the family relation to a mere money relation ... The bourgeoisie cannot exist without constantly revolutionizing the instruments of production, and thereby the relations of production, and with them the whole relations of society ... Constant revolutionizing of production, uninterrupted disturbance of all social conditions, everlasting uncertainty and agitation distinguish the bourgeois epoch from all earlier ones. All fixed, fast-frozen relations, with their train of ancient and venerable prejudices and opinions, are swept away, all new-formed ones become antiquated before they can ossify. All that is solid melts into air, all that is holy is profaned, and man is at last compelled to face with sober senses, his real conditions of life, and his relations with his kind.[5]

It is these revolutionary energies, at once admirable and devastating, that on the one hand lay the material basis for socialism, and on the other hand frustrate that project at every turn. Capitalism sweeps aside all traditional forms of oppression, and in doing so brings humanity face to face with a brutal reality which socialism must then acknowledge and transform.

To grasp one's thought as rooted in the very material conditions it seeks to examine is to be a materialist philosopher, a phrase about which there is more than a hint of paradox. The task of a materialist thought is to calculate into itself that reality – the material world – which is external to thought itself, and which is in some sense more fundamental than it. This is what Marx means by claiming that, in the history of the human species, 'social being' determines consciousness, and not, as the Idealists would have it, vice versa:

> Morality, religion, metaphysics, all the rest of ideology and their corresponding forms of consciousness, thus no longer retain the semblance of independence. They have no history, no development; but men, developing their material production and their material intercourse, alter, along with this their real existence, their thinking and the products of their thinking. Life is not determined by consciousness, but consciousness by life. (GI 47)

Here, then, is Marx's well-known inversion of Hegel, whose topsy-turvy dialectic, of ideas determining social existence, must be set firmly on its materialist feet. For Marx, what we say or think is ultimately determined by what we do. It is historical practices which lie at the bottom of our language games. But some caution is needed here. For what we do as historical beings is of course itself deeply bound up with thought and language; there is no human practice outside the realm of meaning, intention, imagination, as Marx himself insists:

The animal is immediately at one with his life activity. It does not distinguish itself from it. It is *its life activity*. Man makes his life activity itself the object of his will and of his consciousness. He has conscious life activity. It is not a determination with which he directly merges. (EW 328) ... A spider conducts operations that resemble those of a weaver, and a bee puts to shame many an architect in the construction of her cells. But what distinguishes the worst architect from the best of bees is that the architect raises his structure in imagination before he erects it in reality.[6]

Social being gives rise to thought, but is itself caught up in it. Even so, Marx wants to claim that the former is more fundamental – just as he wants to claim that the material 'base' of society gives rise to its cultural, legal, political and ideological 'superstructure':

In the social production of their life, men enter into definite relations that are indispensable and independent of their will, *relations of production* which correspond to a definite stage of development of their material productive *forces*. The sum total of these relations of production constitutes the economic structure of society, the real foundation, on which rises a legal and political superstructure and to which correspond definite forms of social consciousness. The mode of production of material life conditions the social, political and intellectual life process in general. It is not the consciousness of men that determines their being, but on the contrary, their social being that determines their consciousness. (Preface to *A Contribution to the Critique of Political Economy*, SW 182)

Here, then, is Marx's celebrated 'economic theory of history'. His claims about the priorities of social being and consciousness are ontological ones, concerned with the way he takes human beings to be. The base/superstructure doctrine may well be this too: it argues that all social and political forms, and all major historical change, are ultimately determined by conflicts within material production. But the doctrine can also be seen rather more historically, as describing the way in which politics, law, ideology and so on operate in class societies. Marx's point is that in such social orders, precisely because the 'base' of social relations is unjust and contradictory, these forms have the function of ratifying, promoting or concealing this injustice, and so can be said in this sense to be secondary or 'superstructural' to them. There may then be an implication that if the social relations were just, such a superstructure would be unnecessary. We are concerned here, in other words, with the *political* function of ideas in society, not just with their material origin. And this brings us to the Marxist concept of ideology.

The ideas of the ruling class are in every epoch the ruling ideas, i.e. the class which is the ruling *material* force of society, is at the same time its ruling *intellectual* force. The class which has the means of material production at its disposal, has control at the same time over the means of mental production, so that thereby, generally speaking, the ideas of those who lack the means of mental production are subject to it. The ruling ideas are nothing

13

> more than the ideal expression of the dominant material relationships, the dominant material relationships grasped as ideas ... (GI 64)

When philosophy becomes ideology, it tends to distract men and women from historical conflicts by insisting on the primacy of the spiritual, or by offering to resolve these conflicts at a higher, imaginary level. It is for this that Marx upbraids the Hegelians. His own view of history, by contrast,

> ... depends upon our ability to expound the real process of production, starting out from the material production of life itself, and to comprehend the form of intercourse connected with this and created by this mode of production (i.e. civil society in its various stages), as the basis of all history; and to show it in its action as State, to explain all the different theoretical forms and products of consciousness, religion, philosophy, ethics, etc. etc. and trace their origin and growth from that basis; by which means, of course, the whole thing can be depicted in its totality (and therefore, too, the reciprocal action of these various sides on one another). (GI 58)

Unlike Idealist thought, such a materialist viewpoint 'remains constantly on the real *ground* of history':

> [I]t does not explain practice from the idea but explains the formation of ideas from material practice; and accordingly it comes to the conclusion that all forms and products of consciousness cannot be dissolved by mental criticism, by resolution into 'self-consciousness' or transformation into 'apparitions', 'spectres', 'fancies',

etc. but only by the practical overthrow of the actual social relations which gave rise to this idealistic humbug ... (GI 58)

Marx's point is that if key theoretical problems have their anchorage in social contradictions, then they can only be *politically* rather than philosophically resolved. A certain style of philosophizing thus gives rise to a certain 'decentring' of philosophy itself. Like many an anti-philosopher, Marx is trying here to shift the whole terrain on which the discourse is pitched, grasping philosophical puzzles as both symptomatic of a real historical subtext, and as a way of thrusting that subtext out of sight. Much as philosophy would like to dream that it is self-begotten, it has to confront its dependency on that which transcends it. The materialist approach

... shows that history does not end by being resolved into 'self-consciousness' as 'spirit of the spirit', but that in it at each stage there is found a material result: a sum of productive forces, an historically created relation of individuals to nature and to one another, which is handed down to each generation from its predecessor; a mass of productive forces, capital funds and conditions, which, on the one hand, is indeed modified by the new generation, but also on the other prescribes for it its conditions of life and gives it a definite development, a special character. It shows that circumstances make men just as much as men make circumstances. (GI 59)

Humanity, then, is not just the determined product of its material conditions; if it were, how could Marx hope that it might one day transform them? He is not a 'mechanical' materialist like, say, Thomas Hobbes, viewing consciousness as the mere reflex of circumstance, but an *historical* materialist in the sense that he wishes to explain the origin, character and function of ideas in terms of the historical conditions to which they belong.

He seems to have forgotten, however, that not all philosophy is necessarily Idealist. His own thought is not, and neither was that of the great bourgeois materialists of the French Enlightenment from whom he learnt. Nor, for that matter, is all ideology 'Idealist'. Even so, Marx's view of Idealist philosophy is an original one: he sees it as a form of fantasy, striving to attain in the mind what cannot yet be achieved in historical reality. And in this sense, the resolution of historical contradictions would spell the death of philosophical speculation. But this is true too of Marx's own thought. There would be no place for Marxist philosophy in a truly communist society, since such theory exists purely to help bring such a society into being. Indeed, in its anti-utopian way, Marx's work has strikingly little to say about what that future state of affairs would actually look like. His thought, like all radical political theory, is thus finally self-abolishing. And this is perhaps the most profound sense in which it is historical.

ANTHROPOLOGY

(P)ost) modern thought tends to be anti-foundational-ist, suspecting any objective ground to our existence as some arbitrary fiction of our own. Marx, by contrast, is a more classical or traditional thinker, for whom the ground of our being is that shared form of material nature he names 'species-being'. Like the phrase 'human nature', this concept hovers ambiguously between description and pre-scription, fact and value, an account of how we are and how we ought to be. We are naturally social animals, dependent upon each other for our very survival, yet this must become a political value as well as an anthropological fact. As an historicist thinker, Marx is out to rescue human institutions from the false eternality with which metaphysi-cal thought has endowed them; what was historically created can always be historically changed. But he is also, somewhat paradoxically, a sort of Aristotelian essentialist, who holds that there is a human nature or essence, and that the just society would be one in which this nature was allowed to come into its own. How, then, does he resolve this apparent discrepancy in his thought?

He does so, like Hegel before him, by seeing change, development, as of the essence of humanity. It is of our nature to realize our powers; but what kind of powers are in question, and under what conditions we actualize them, is an historically specific affair. For the young Marx of the

17

Economic and Philosophical Manuscripts, we are human in so far as we share a specific kind of 'species-being' with our fellow human creatures:

> The *human* essence of nature exists only for *social* man; for only here does nature exist for him as a *bond* with other *men*, as his existence for others and their existence for him, as the vital element of human reality; only here does it exist as the *basis* of his own *human* existence. Only here has his *natural* existence become his *human* existence and nature become man for him. *Society* is therefore the perfected unity in essence of man with nature, the true resurrection of nature, the realized naturalism of man and the realized humanism of nature ... It is above all necessary to avoid once more establishing 'society' as an abstraction over against the individual. The individual *is* the *social being*. His vital expression – even when it does not appear in the direct form of a *communal* expression, conceived in association with other men – is therefore an expression and confirmation of *social life*. Man's individual and species-life are not two *distinct things* ... (EW 350)

Does this species-being have an end or goal? Is Marx a teleological thinker? In one sense yes, in another sense no. For the end of our species-being, in a kind of creative tautology, consists just in realizing itself. For Marx, as for other Romantic radicals, there is or should be no ultimate point to human existence beyond its self-delighting development:

> When communist *workmen* gather together, their

immediate aim is instruction, propaganda, etc. But at the same time they acquire a new need – the need for society – and what appears as a means has become an end. This practical development can be most strikingly observed in the gatherings of French socialist workers. Smoking, eating and drinking, etc., are no longer means of creating links between people. Company, association, conversation, which in its turn has society as its goal, is good enough for them. The brotherhood of man is not a hollow phrase, it is a reality, and the nobility of man shines forth upon us from their work-worn figures. (EW 365)

This Romantic notion of a nature whose self-development is an end in itself stands opposed to two other powerful thought-forms of Marx's day. The first is that brand of metaphysical reasoning which would summon human activity to account before some higher tribunal: of duty, morality, religious sanctions, the Absolute Idea. Marx is profoundly hostile to such metaphysics, though he is a profound moralist in his own right. It is just that for him morality actually *consists* in this process of unfolding our creative powers and capacities, not in some law set above it or some august set of ends pitched beyond it. There is no need to *justify* this dynamic, any more than we need to justify a smile or a song; it just belongs to our common nature.

But this ethic also finds itself in conflict with that form of *instrumental* reason for which individuals exist for the sake of some greater goal: the political state, for example, or – as in the dominant Utilitarian thought of Marx's era – the promotion of universal happiness. This means/ends reasoning is the form of rationality which Marx believes to hold sway in class societies, in which the energies of the majority are made instrumental to the profit of the few. In capitalist society,

> labour, life activity, productive life itself appears to man only as a *means* for the satisfaction of a need, the need to preserve physical existence. But productive life is species-life. It is life-producing life. The whole character of a species, its species-character, resides in the nature of its life activity, and free conscious activity constitutes the species-character of man. [In capitalism], life itself appears only as a *means of life*. (EW 328)

In class society, the individual is forced to convert what is least functional about herself – her self-realizing species-being – into a mere tool of material survival.

It is not, of course, that Marx disowns such instrumental reasoning altogether. Without it, there could be no rational action at all; and his own revolutionary politics necessarily involve the fitting of means to ends. But one of the many ironies of his thought is that this is in the service of constructing a society in which men and women would be allowed to flourish as radical ends in themselves. It is just because he values the individual so deeply that Marx rejects a social order which, while trumpeting the value of individualism in theory, in practice reduces men and women to anonymously interchangeable units.

If we were asked to characterize Marx's ethics, then, we might do worse than call them 'aesthetic'. For the aesthetic is traditionally that form of human practice which requires no utilitarian justification, but which furnishes its own goals, grounds and rationales. It is an exercise of self-fulfilling energy for the mere sake of it; and socialism for Marx is just the practical movement to bring about a state of affairs in which something like this would be available to as many individuals as possible. Where art was, there shall humanity be. This is why he wants a society in which labour would be automated as far as possible, so that men and women (capitalists as well as workers) would no longer be reduced to mere tools of production, and would be free instead to develop their personalities in more fully rounded ways. Socialism for him depends crucially upon shortening the working-day, to allow this general flourishing to become available:

> Freedom in this field [of labour] can only consist in socialized man, the associated producers, rationally regulating their interchange with Nature; and achieving this with the least expenditure of energy and under conditions most favourable to, and worthy of, their human nature. But it nonetheless remains a realm of necessity. Beyond it begins that development of human energy which is an end in itself, the true realm of freedom, which, however, can blossom forth only with this realm of necessity as its basis. The shortening of the working-day is its basic prerequisite. (C Vol. 3 85)

Another way of putting the point is to claim that Marx wants to liberate the 'use-value' of human beings from its enthralment to 'exchange-value'. An object for him is a sensuous thing which we should use and enjoy with respect to its specific qualities; this is what he means by its 'use-value'. Under capitalist conditions, however, objects are reduced to commodities: they exist merely for the sake of their exchange-value, of being bought and sold. And as far as that goes, any two commodities of the same value are reduced to an abstract equality with each other. Their specific sensuous features are thus damagingly ignored, as difference is dominated by identity.

But this is equally true of human beings under the same social system. Under market conditions, individuals confront each other as abstract, interchangeable entities; working people become commodities, selling their labour power to the highest bidder; and the capitalist does not care what he produces as long as it makes a profit. What goes for the economic realm is also true of the political arena: the bourgeois state regards its citizens as abstractly equal when it comes, say, to the voting booth, but only in a way which suppresses and conceals their specific social inequalities. The aim of socialist democracy is to heal this fissure between the political form and the social content, so that our presence within the political state, as participating citizens, would be our presence as actual individuals:

> Only when real, individual man resumes the abstract citizen into himself and as an individual man has become a *species-being* in his empirical life, his individual work and his individual relationships, only when man has recognized and organized his *forces propres* as social forces so that social force is no longer separated from him in the form of political force, only then will human emancipation be completed. (EW 234)

Just as Marx wants to abolish commodity exchange in the

economic sphere, so that production becomes for use rather than for profit, so he wishes to 'de-commodify' the human personality, emancipating the wealth of sensuous individual development from the abstract, utilitarian logic in which it is currently imprisoned. Under capitalism, our very senses are turned into commodities, so that only with the abolition of private property would the human body be liberated and the human senses come into their own:

> The supersession of private property is therefore the complete emancipation of all human senses and attributes; but it is this emancipation precisely because these senses and attributes have become *human*, subjectively as well as objectively. The eye has become a *human* eye, just as its object has become a social, human object, made by man for man. The senses have therefore become *theoreticians* in their immediate praxis. They relate to the thing for its own sake, but the thing itself is an *objective human* relation to itself and to man, and vice versa. Need or enjoyment have therefore lost their *egoistic* nature, and nature has lost its mere *utility* in the sense that its use has become *human* use. (EW 352)

Marx's political anthropology is rooted in a very broad conception of labour, which is to say, in the notion of the human body as the source of social life.

As social life grows more complex, labour becomes inevitably more specialized, with different forms of it divided out between different producers; this is what Marx calls the division of labour. This is a necessary way of developing and refining the forces of production; but it also involves for Marx a kind of alienation, in which human powers are realized in cripplingly one-sided ways, as against his ideal of the 'all-round' individual who deploys a prodigal wealth of talent. The division of labour is thus another instance of the divorce in class society between the individual and the universal, as the full potential of our species-being dwindles to some single function such as the mechanical labour of the factory worker:

> ... the division of labour offers us the first example of how, as long as man remains in natural society, that is, as long as a cleavage exists between the particular and the common interest, as long, therefore, as activity is not voluntary, but naturally, divided, man's own deed becomes an alien power opposed to him, which enslaves him instead of being controlled by him. For as soon as the distribution of labour comes into being, each man has a particular, exclusive sphere of activity, which is forced upon him and from which he cannot escape. He is a hunter, a fisherman, a herdsman, or a critical critic, and must remain so if he does not want to lose his means of livelihood; while in communist society, where nobody has one exclusive sphere of activity but each can become accomplished in any branch he wishes, society regulates the general production and thus makes it possible for me to do one thing today and another tomorrow, to hunt in the morning, fish in the afternoon, rear cattle in the evening, criticize after dinner, just as I have a mind, without ever becoming fisherman, herdsman or critic. (GI 54)

This, famously or notoriously, is one of Marx's few frankly utopian speculations.

There are, inevitably, many problems with Marx's political ethics, as there are with any other sort of ethics. Is this notion of a freely self-fashioning human subject perhaps just a more generous-spirited version of the bourgeois, patriarchal model of man as a strenuous self-producer? Is Marx's ideal human being a kind of proletarian Promethean? To what extent is this a left-wing version of the middle-class ideal of a limitless, Faustian realization of wealth, which treats the self as one's own possession? One might find a rather too relentless activism about the doctrine, which undervalues what Wordsworth called 'wise passiveness' or Keats named 'negative capability'. Are we to realize *all* of our powers and capacities? What about those which seem morbid or destructive? Perhaps Marx considers that our powers become destructive only by virtue of being constrained, in which case he is surely mistaken. And how are we to discriminate between our more positive and negative capacities, if we have no criteria beyond this historically relative process itself by which to do so? 'All-round' development may seem to some inferior to the cultivation of a single creative talent, just as self-denial may appear to some more commendable than self-expression.

Some of these critical points can be countered. Marx, good materialist that he was, plainly did not believe that human self-development could be unlimited; he was alert to the limitations of our estate as well as to its potentials:

> *Man* is directly a *natural being*. As a natural being and as a living natural being he is on the one hand equipped with *natural powers*, with *vital powers*, he is an *active* natural being ... On the other hand, as a natural,

corporeal, sensuous, objective being he is a *suffering*, conditioned and limited being, like animals and plants. That is to say, the *objects* of his drives exist outside him as *objects* independent of him; but these objects are objects of his *need*, essential objects, indispensable to the exercise and confirmation of his essential powers. (EW 389)

Marx may have overrated production, but he certainly did not narrow the term to its economic sense. On the contrary, he thought it a spiritually impoverishing feature of capitalism that it did precisely that. 'Production' for him is a richly capacious concept, equivalent to 'self-actualization'; and to this extent savouring a peach or enjoying a string quartet are aspects of our self-actualization as much as building dams or churning out coat-hangers:

... when the limited bourgeois form is stripped away, what is wealth other than the universality of individual needs, capacities, pleasures, productive forces etc. created through universal exchange? The full development of human mastery over the forces of nature, those of so-called nature as well as of humanity's own nature? The absolute working out of [the human being's] creative potentialities with no presupposition other than the previous historic development, which makes this totality of development, i.e. the development of all human powers as such the end in itself, not as measured on a *predetermined* yardstick? Where he does not reproduce himself in one specificity, but produces his totality? Strives not to remain something he has become, but is in the absolute movement of becoming?[7]

Our species-being, then, is naturally productive, concerned with unfolding its powers by transforming the world:

> The practical creation of an *objective* world, the *fashioning* of inorganic nature, is proof that man is a conscious species-being, i.e. a being which treats the species as its own essential being or itself as a species-being. It is true that animals also produce ... But they produce only their own immediate needs or those of their young; they produce one-sidedly, whereas man produces universally; they produce only when immediate physical need compels them to do so, while man produces even when he is free from physical need and truly produces only in freedom from such need. (EW 329)

We are free when, like artists, we produce without the goad of physical necessity; and it is this nature which for Marx is the essence of all individuals. In developing my own individual personality through fashioning a world, I am also realizing what it is that I have most deeply in common with others, so that individual and species-being are ultimately one. My product is my existence for the other, and presupposes the other's existence for me. This for Marx is an ontological truth, which follows from the kind of creatures we are; but it is possible for certain forms of social life to drive a wedge between these two dimensions of the self, individual and communal, and this, in effect, is what the young Marx means by *alienation*. In one sense, such a fissure always exists, since it is of the essence of the human being that he can 'objectify' his own nature, stand off from it, and this is at the root of our freedom. But in class society, the objects produced by the majority of men and women are appropriated by the minority who own and control the means of production; and this means that they are now no longer able to recognize themselves in the world that they have created. Their self-realization is no longer an end in itself, but becomes purely instrumental to the self-development of others:

> This fact simply means that the object that labour produces, its product, stands opposed to it as *something alien*, as a power *independent* of the producer. The product of labour is labour embodied and made material in an object, it is the objectification of labour ... In the sphere of political economy this realization of labour appears as a *loss of reality* for the worker, objectification *as loss of and bondage to the object*, and appropriation as *estrangement, as alienation* ... Estranged labour not only (1) estranges nature from man and (2) estranges man from himself, from his own active function, from his vital activity; because of this it also estranges man from his *species*. It turns his *species-life* into a means for his individual life. (EW 324, 328)

The worker, as Marx comments, feels at home only when he is not working, and not at home when he is working. So alienation is a multiple process, divorcing the worker from nature, from her product and the labour process itself, from her own body, but also from that communal life-activity which makes of her a truly human being. 'In general,' Marx writes, 'the proposition that man is estranged from his species-being means that man is estranged from the others and that all are estranged from man's essence' (EW 330).

In suffering a 'loss of reality', the producers ironically strengthen by their labour the very regime which brings this about:

> ... the more the worker exerts himself in his work, the more powerful the alien, objective world becomes which he brings into being over against himself, the poorer he and his inner world become, and the less they belong to him. It is the same in religion. The more man puts into God, the less he retains within himself. The worker places his life in the object; but now it no longer belongs to him, but to the object. The greater his activity, therefore, the fewer objects the worker possesses. What the product of his labour is, he is not. Therefore, the greater this product, the less he is himself. The alienation of the worker means not only that his labour becomes an object, an *external* existence, but that it exists *outside him*, independently of him and alien to him, and begins to confront him as an autonomous power; that the life which he has bestowed on the object confronts him as hostile and alien. (EW 324)

The labourer's products slip from his control, assume an autonomy of their own, and come to exert that quasi-magical power over him which Marx will later term 'the fetishism of commodities'. A commodity for Marx is a product which can exchange equally with another because it embodies the same amount of labour. As he explains in *Capital*,

Let us take two commodities, e.g. iron and corn. The proportions in which they are exchangeable, whatever those proportions may be, can always be represented by an equation in which a given quantity of corn is equated to some quantity of iron ... What does this equation tell us? It tells us that in two different things – in 1 quarter of corn and x cwt of iron, there exists in equal quantities something common to both. The two things must therefore be equal to a third, which in itself is neither the one nor the other. Each of them, as far as it is exchange value, must be reducible to this third ... This common 'something' cannot be either a geometrical, a chemical, or any other natural property of commodities. Such properties claim our attention only in as far as they affect the utility of those commodities, make them use-values. But the exchange of commodities is evidently an act characterized by a total abstraction from use-value ... As use-values, commodities are, above all, of different qualities, but as exchange-values they are merely different quantities, and consequently do not contain an atom of use-value. If, then, we leave out of consideration the use-value of commodities, they have only one property left, that of being products of labour. (C Vol. 1 37)

Commodities for Marx are thus duplicitous entities living a double life, since what actually makes them commodities is curiously independent of their material properties. They exist purely to be exchanged; and one commodity, despite all sensuous appearances, is exactly equal to any other commodity which embodies the same quantity of labour power. But a commodity is therefore an entirely abstract phenomenon, which sets up relations with other commodities in ways quite independent of the concrete life of their producers:

> A commodity, therefore, is a mysterious thing, simply because in it the social character of men's labour appears to them as an objective character stamped upon the product of that labour; because the relation of the producers to the sum total of their own labour is presented to them as social relation, existing not between themselves but between the products of their labour … [The] existence of things *qua* commodities, and the value-relation between the products of labour which stamps them as commodities, have absolutely no connection with their physical properties and with the material relations arising therefrom … It is a definite social relation between men, that assumes, in their eyes, the fantastic form of a relation between things. In order … to find an analogy, we must have recourse to the mist-enveloped regions of the religious world. In that world the productions of the human brain appear as independent beings endowed with life, and entering into relations both with one another and with the human race. So it is in the world of commodities with the products of men's hands. This I call Fetishism which attaches itself to the products of labour, so soon as they are produced as commodities, and which is therefore inseparable from the production of commodities. (C Vol. 1 72)

Capitalism, in short, is a world in which subject and object are reversed – a realm in which one is subjected to and determined by one's own productions, which return in opaque, imperious form to hold sway over one's existence. The human subject creates an object, which then becomes a pseudo-subject able to reduce its own creator to a manipulated thing. When capital employs labour rather than vice versa, the dead come to assume a vampiric power over the living, since capital itself is simply 'dead' or stored labour:

> The less you eat, drink, buy books, go to the theatre, go dancing, go drinking, think, love, theorize, sing, paint, fence, etc., the more you save and the greater will become the treasure which neither moths nor maggots can consume – your *capital*. The less you *are*, the less you give expression to your life, the more you *have*, the greater is your *alienated* life and the more you store up of your estranged life … everything which you are unable to do, your money can do for you … (EW 361)

This process of reification, in which animate and inanimate are inverted and the dead tyrannize over the living, is particularly evident in the 'universal commodity', money:

> The stronger the power of my money, the stronger am I. The properties of money are my, the possessor's, properties and essential powers. Therefore what I *am* and what I *can do* is by no means determined by my individuality. I *am* ugly, but I can buy the *most beautiful* woman. Which means to say that I am not *ugly*, for the effect of *ugliness*, its repelling power, is destroyed by money. As an individual, I am *lame*, but money procures

32

me twenty-four legs. Consequently, I am not lame. I am a wicked, dishonest, unscrupulous and stupid individual, but money is respected, and so also is its owner. Money is the highest good, and consequently its owner is also *good*. (EW 377)

Money, Marx comments, is 'the universal whore, the universal pimp of men and peoples', a kind of garbled language in which all human and natural qualities are scrambled and inverted and anything can be magically transformed into anything else.

For men and women to have their world, their sensuous bodies, their life-activity and their being-in-common restored to them is what Marx means by communism. Communism is just the kind of political set-up which would allow us to reappropriate our confiscated being, those powers alienated from us under class society. If the means of production were to be commonly owned and democratically controlled, then the world we create together would belong to us in common, and the self-production of each could become part of the self-realization of all.

HISTORY

If Marx is a philosopher, what is he a philosopher of? Certainly nothing as grandiose as 'human existence', but also nothing as narrow as political economy. His thought is not intended as some kind of cosmic theory which like, say, religion is meant to account for all features of human life. It is true that his collaborator Frederick Engels evolved a vastly ambitious theory known as dialectical materialism, which seeks to weave together everything from physics and biology to history and society. But Marx's own writing represents a rather more modest, restricted enterprise, which aims to identify, and work to dismantle, the major social contradictions which at present prevent us from living what he would see as a truly human life, in all the wealth of our bodily and spiritual powers. He has very little to say of what would happen then, since for him this process would be the beginnings of human history proper, which lies beyond our present language. Everything that has happened to date is for him mere 'pre-history' – the succession of various forms of class society. And since Marx's own work belongs to this epoch, inevitably dependent on its thought forms and life models, it cannot, by its own historicist logic, seek to leap over it to imagine some sort of utopia. Marx is resolutely hostile to such utopianism, seeing his own task not as drawing up ideal blueprints for the future, but as analysing and unlocking the real contradictions of the present. He is not looking for a perfect state, a phrase which for him would be a contradiction in terms.

But that is not to say that Marx is just a political theorist of the present. The contradictions which he sees as preventing us from getting a true history off the ground, in all of its richness, enjoyment and individual variety, are for him part of a much more lengthy narrative. He is thus not primarily a political economist or sociologist, or – as we have seen – in the first place a philosopher. Rather, he is offering us a theory of history itself, or more precisely a theory of the dynamics of major historical change. It is this philosophy which has become known as historical materialism.

How, then, did Marx view history as developing? It is sometimes thought that what is central to his outlook here is the notion of social class. But Marx did not discover this idea, and it is not his most vital concept. It would be more accurate to claim that the idea of class *struggle* lies closer to the heart of his work: the doctrine that different social classes exist in a state of mutual antagonism on account of their conflicting material interests. As he writes in *Communist Manifesto*: 'The history of all hitherto existing society is the history of class struggles' (SW 35). But even this sweeping pronouncement does not quite lead us to the core of his thought. For we can always ask *why* social classes should live in this state of permanent warfare; and the answer for Marx has to do with the history of material production.

His key concept here is that of a 'mode of production', by which he means an historically specific combination of certain *forces* of production with certain social *relations* of production. By 'forces' he means the various means of production available to a society, along with human labour power. A power loom or a computer is a productive force, capable of producing value; but such material forces are only ever invented, developed and deployed within the framework of particular social relations of production, by which Marx refers mainly to the relations between those who own and control the means of production, and those non-owners whose labour power is placed at their disposal. On one reading of Marx, history progresses by the forces and relations of production entering into contradiction with each other:

> At a certain stage of their development, the material productive forces of society enter into contradiction with the existing relations of production, or – what is but a legal expression of the same thing – with the property relations within which they have been at work hitherto. From forms of development of the productive forces, these relations turn into their fetters. Then begins an epoch of social revolution. (Preface to *A Contribution to the Critique of Political Economy*, SW 182)

It is by this mechanism that one mode of production gives way to another. The first such mode for Marx is the 'tribal':

> It corresponds to the undeveloped stage of production, at which a people lives by hunting and fishing, by the rearing of beasts or, in the highest stage, agriculture. In the latter case it presupposes a great mass of unculti- vated stretches of land. The division of labour is at this stage still very elementary and is confined to a further

36

extension of the natural division of labour existing in the family. The social structure is, therefore, limited to an extension of the family: patriarchal family chieftains, below them the members of the tribe, finally slaves. (GI 44)

From this gradually evolves the 'ancient' mode of production,

which proceeds especially from the union of several tribes into a *city* by agreement or by conquest, and which is still accompanied by slavery. Beside communal ownership we already find movable, and later also immovable, private property developing, but as an abnormal form subordinate to communal ownership. The citizens hold power over their labouring slaves only in their community, and on this account alone, therefore, they are bound to the form of communal ownership ... the whole structure of society based on this communal ownership, and with it the power of the people, decays in the same measure as, in particular, immovable private property evolves. (GI 44)

From this eventually follows the feudal mode of production:

Like tribal and communal ownership, [feudal property] is based again on a community; but the directly producing class standing over against it is not, as in the case of the ancient community, the slaves, but the enserfed small peasantry. As soon as feudalism is fully developed, there also arises antagonism to the towns. The hierarchical structure of landownership, and the armed bodies of retainers associated with it, gave the nobility power over the serfs. This feudal organization was, just as much as the ancient communal ownership, an association against a subjected producing class; but the form of association and the relation to the direct producers were different because of the different conditions of production. (GI 45)

Along with the feudal landed estates grew up mercantile guilds in the towns, with small-scale production and scant division of labour. But the social relations of feudalism, with its restricted guild system, end up holding back the development of the emerging middle classes of the towns, who finally break through these constrictions in a political revolution and release the forces of production on an epic scale. Later however, as a fully fledged industrial capitalist class, this same bourgeoisie finds itself unable to continue to develop those forces without generating extreme inequalities, economic slumps, unemployment, artificial scarcity and the destruction of capital. It will thus lay the ground for its own supersession by the working class, whose task is to seize control of the means of production and operate them in the interests of all:

As soon as this process [of the rise of capitalism] has sufficiently decomposed the old society from top to bottom, as soon as the labourers are turned into proletarians, their means of labour into capital, as soon as the capitalist mode of production stands on its own feet, then the further socialization of labour and further transformation of the land and other means of production into socially exploited, and, therefore, common

means of production, as well as the further expropriation
of private property, takes a new form. That which is now
to be expropriated is no longer the labourer working for
himself, but the capitalist exploiting many labourers.
This expropriation is accomplished by the action of the
immanent laws of capitalistic production itself, by the
centralization of capital. One capitalist always kills many.
('Historical Tendency of Capitalist Accumulation', SW
236)

Capitalism, in other words, prepares the way for its own
negation, by socializing labour and centralizing capital:

Hand in hand with this centralization, or this expropriation of many capitalists by few, develop, on an ever-
extending scale, the cooperative form of the labour-
process, the conscious technical application of science,
the methodical cultivation of the soil, the transformation
of the instruments of labour into instruments of labour
only usable in common, the economizing of all means of
production by their use as the means of production of
combined, socialized labour, the entanglement of all
peoples in the net of the world market, and with this, the
international character of the capitalistic regime. (Ibid.,
SW 236)

It is capitalism, then, which brings its own collective
antagonist – the workers – into being, giving birth in a wry
irony to its own gravediggers:

Along with the constantly diminishing number of the
magnates of capital, who usurp and monopolize all
advantages of this process of transformation, grows the

mass of misery, oppression, slavery, degradation, exploitation; but with this too grows the revolt of the working class, a class always increasing in numbers, and disciplined, united, organized by the very mechanism of the process of capitalist production itself. The monopoly of capital becomes a fetter upon the mode of production, which has flourished and sprung up along with, and under it. Centralization of the means of production and socialization of labour at last reach a point where they become incompatible with their capitalist integument. This integument is burst asunder. The knell of capitalist private property sounds. The expropriators are expropriated. (Ibid., SW 237)

Stated as such, the whole process of proletarian revolution sounds implausibly automatic. On this version of Marx's thought, ruling classes rise and fall according to their capacity to develop the forces of production, and one mode of production – primitive communism, slavery, feudalism, capitalism – thus mutates by its own immanent logic into another. We have here a kind of historicized verison of Marx's anthropology: what is positive is human development, and what is negative is whatever impedes that process. But it is not quite clear how to square this model with those parts of Marx's work which suggest that what is central is not the forces but the *relations* of production, as ruling classes develop the forces of production in their own interests and for their own exploitative purposes. Since this leads to the deprivation of the subordinate classes, political revolution on this model comes about directly through class struggle, not because of some general trans-historical impulse to free the productive forces of their social constraints. It is class conflict which is the dynamic of history, but one rooted in the business of material production.

Marx's particular attention, not least in his major work *Capital*, is naturally to the mode of production of his own day. Under this system, the worker, who owns nothing but his or her capacity to labour (or labour power), is compelled to sell that capacity to an owner of capital, who then puts it to work for his own profit. Human beings themselves are turned into replaceable commodities in the marketplace. The capitalist pays for the hire of the worker's labour power in that exchange of commodities we know as wages – wages being the cost of what the worker needs to 'reproduce' her labour power, i.e. the goods necessary for her to stay alive and keep working. But labour power, since it is never a fixed object but a matter of human energy and potential, is a peculiarly open-ended, indeterminate sort of commodity; and in putting it to work, the capitalist is able to reap from it more value, in the form of goods produced and sold, than it is necessary to pay to the worker. This process, which Marx calls the extraction of 'surplus value' from the working class, is the key to the exploitative nature of capitalist social relations; but because the exchange of wages for labour appears an equitable one, this exploitation is necessarily concealed by the very routine workings of the system itself.

The capitalist system, however, is a competitive one, in which each manufacturer must strive to expand his capital or go under. One result of this in Marx's view is a tendency for the rate of profit to fall, leading to the notorious recessions which have characterized the system to date. The system's contradictions thus sharpen, and along with them the class struggle itself, since it is in the interests of capital to appropriate as much as possible of the fruits of its workers' labour in the shape of profit, and in the interests of the workers to claw back as much of the proceeds of their own labour as they can. For Marx, the only final resolution of this deadlock is socialist revolution, as the working class expropriates capital itself, asserts its collective control over it, and places it in the service of the needs of all rather than the benefit of a few.

Marxism is not some form of moralism, which denounces the capitalists as villains and idealizes the workers. It aims rather for a 'scientific' theory of historical change, in which no ruling class can be said to be unequivocally positive or negative. On one reading, a class is 'progressive' if it is still able to develop the forces of production – which may be taken to mean that slavery was in its day a progressive mode. This clearly offends our sense of justice; but Marx himself would sometimes seem to have regarded concepts like justice as mere bourgeois ideology masking exploitation, even if his own work is ironically fuelled by a passionate desire for a just society. The bourgeoisie may be an obstacle to freedom, justice and universal wellbeing today; but in its heyday it was a revolutionary force which overthrew its own feudal antagonists, which bequeathed the very ideas of justice and liberty to its socialist successors, and which developed the forces of production to the point where socialism itself might become a feasible project. For without the material and spiritual wealth which capitalism has developed, socialism itself would not be possible. A socialism which needs to develop the forces of production from the ground up, without the benefit of a capitalist class which has accomplished this task for it, will tend to end up as that authoritarian form of state power we know as Stalinism. And a socialism which fails to inherit from the middle class a rich legacy of liberal freedoms and civic institutions will simply reinforce that autocracy. The bourgeoisie may have done what they did from the least creditable of motives, that of individual profit; but taken collectively this proved a remarkably efficient way of bringing the forces of production to the point where, given a socialist reorganization of them, they could provide the resources to wipe out poverty and deprivation throughout the world.

But the achievement of the revolutionary middle class was not just material. In bringing the individual to new heights of complex development, it also unfolded a human wealth to which socialism would be enduringly indebted. Marxism is not a question of thinking up some fine new social ideals, but rather of asking why it is that the fine ideals we already have, have proved structurally incapable of being realized for everyone. It is out to create the material conditions in which this might become possible; and one such condition is the fact that the bourgeoisie is the first genuinely *universal* social class, which breaks down all parochial barriers and breeds the kind of truly global communication which might form the basis of an international socialist community.

A truly dialectical theory of class history, then, strives to grasp its emancipatory and oppressive aspects together, as elements of a single logic. Marx summarizes this view in a typically eloquent passage:

> In our days, everything seems pregnant with its contrary. Machinery gifted with the wonderful power of shortening and fructifying human labour, we behold starving and overworking it. The new-fangled sources of wealth, by some strange weird spell, are turned into sources of want. The victories of art seem bought by the loss of character. At the same pace that mankind masters nature, man seems to become enslaved to other men or to his own infamy. Even the pure light of science seems unable to shine but on the dark background of ignorance. All our invention and progress seem to result in endowing material forces with intellectual life, and stultifying human life into a material force. This antagonism between modern industry and science on the one hand, between misery and dissolution on the other hand; this antagonism between the productive forces and the social relations of our epoch is a fact, palpable, overwhelming, and not to be controverted. (*The People's Paper*, 1856)

Irony, inversion, chiasmus, contradiction lie at the heart of Marx's conception of things. In accumulating the greatest wealth that history has ever witnessed, the capitalist class has done so within the context of social relations which have left most of its subordinates hungry, wretched and oppressed. It has also brought to birth a social order in which, in the antagonisms of the marketplace, each individual is set against the other – in which aggression, domination, rivalry, warfare and imperialist exploitation

44

are the order of the day, rather than cooperation and comradeship. The history of capitalism is the history of possessive individualism, in which each self-owning human being is locked off from others in his solipsistic space, seeing his fellows only as tools to be used to promote his appetitive interests. But it is not that Marx is opposed to individualism, wishing to sink it in some faceless collectivity. On the contrary, his aim is to re-establish communal bonds between men and women *at the level of* their fully developed individual powers. As he puts it in the *Communist Manifesto*, the free development of each must become the condition for the free development of all. And this can be achieved only through the abolition of private property.

There are, inevitably, a number of problems with this audacious, imaginative theory. For one thing, it is not exactly clear what Marx means by social class. It is a wry joke among his commentators that just as he is about to examine the concept fully, his work breaks off. But it is clear that he sees class primarily as an economic category: it denotes, roughly speaking, those who stand in the same relation as each other to the mode of production, so that, for example, small independent producers such as peasants and artisans can be classified together as 'petty bourgeois', whereas those who must sell their labour power to another are proletarians. Does this, then, make a millionaire film star and a garbage collector both part of the working class? Or should political, cultural and ideological factors be allowed to enter into what we mean by the category? What are the relations or non-relations between social class and other human groupings, national, ethnic or sexual, to which Marx himself gives much less attention? Must a class be conscious of itself as such to be, properly speaking, a class? It is a question which Marx considers in his discussion of the French peasantry in *The Eighteenth Brumaire of Louis Bonaparte*:

> The small-holding peasants form a vast mass, the members of which live in similar conditions but without entering into manifold relations with one another. Their mode of production isolates them from one another instead of bringing them into mutual intercourse … In so far as millions of families live under economic conditions of existence that separate their mode of life, their interests and their culture from those of other classes, and put them in hostile opposition to the latter, they form a class. In so far as there is merely a local interconnection among these small-holding peasants, and the identity of their interests begets no community, no national bond and no political organization among them, they do not form a class. (SW 172)

As for the theory of historical change: if Marx really does hold that the point is always and everywhere to *develop* the productive forces, then he is vulnerable to an ecological critique. We may ask, too, whether he regards this historical dialectic as inevitable. In the *Communist Manifesto* he declares that the downfall of the bourgeoisie and the victory of the proletariat 'are alike inevitable'; and in *Capital* he writes of the laws of capitalism as 'working with iron necessity towards inevitable results' (C Vol. 1 9). Elsewhere, however, Marx pours scorn on the idea that there is an entity called History which operates in deterministic style through human beings:

> ... *History* does *nothing*, it 'possesses no immense wealth', it 'wages no battles'. It is *man*, real living man, that does all that, that possesses and fights; 'history' is not a person apart, using man as a means for *its own* particular ends; history is *nothing but* the activity of man pursuing his aim ...[8]

He also rejects the idea that the various historical modes of production must follow upon one another in some rigidly determined way. Nor does he seem to think that the productive forces are always inexorably expanding. Anyway, if the overthrow of capitalism is inevitable, why should the working class not just sit back and wait for it to happen rather than organizing to bring it politically about? One might claim, as Marx seems to, that it is inevitable that the working class will grow to consciousness of its plight and act to change it, so that its 'free' action is somehow calculated into the broader deterministic narrative. Some Christians have tried in similar ways to resolve the apparent discrepancy between free will and divine providence. But in practice, when he is analysing particular political situations, Marx would seem to believe that political revolution depends on the struggle of contending social forces, and the outcome of this is in no sense historically guaranteed. There are, to be sure, historical laws; but these are the results of concerted human action, not of some destiny grandly independent of it. As Marx famously puts it in *The Eighteenth Brumaire*:

> Men make their own history, but they do not make it just as they please; they do not make it under circumstances chosen by themselves, but under circumstances

directly encountered, given and transmitted from the past. The tradition of all the dead generations weighs like a nightmare on the brains of the living ... The social revolution of the nineteenth century cannot draw its poetry from the past, but only from the future. It cannot begin with itself before it has stripped off all superstitions in regard to the past. Earlier revolutions required recollections of past world history in order to drug themselves concerning their own content. In order to arrive at its own content, the revolution of the nineteenth century must let the dead bury their dead. (SW 97)

POLITICS

If Marx is indeed some sort of philosopher, he differs from most such thinkers in regarding his reflections, however abstruse, as being ultimately practical – as being wholly at the service of actual political forces, and indeed as a kind of political force in themselves. This is the celebrated Marxist thesis of the unity of theory and practice – though one might add that one aim of Marx's theory is to arrive at a social condition in which thought would no longer need to be simply instrumental, geared to some practical end, and could be enjoyed instead as a pleasure in itself.

Marx's political doctrine is a revolutionary one – 'revolution' for him being defined less by the speed, suddenness or violence of a process of social change (though he does seem to consider that insurrectionary force will be involved in constructing socialism), than by the fact that it involves the ousting of one possessing class and its replacement by another. And this is a process which might clearly take a good deal of time to accomplish. We can note here the peculiar feature of socialism: that it involves the working class coming to power, but in doing so creating the conditions in which all classes may be abolished. Once the means of production are communally owned and controlled, classes themselves will finally disappear:

All the preceding classes that got the upper hand, sought to fortify their already acquired status by subjecting society at large to their conditions of appropriation. The proletarians cannot become masters of the productive forces of society, except by abolishing their own previous mode of appropriation, and thereby also every other previous mode of appropriation. They have nothing of their own to secure and fortify; their mission is to destroy all previous securities for, and insurances of, individual property. (*Communist Manifesto*, SW 45)

Or as Marx puts it in the idiom of his earlier writings:

A class must be formed which has *radical chains*, a class in civil society which is not a class of civil society, a class which is the dissolution of all classes, a sphere of society which has a universal character because its sufferings are universal, and which does not claim a *particular redress* because the wrong which is done to it is not a *particular wrong* but *wrong in general*. There must be formed a sphere of society which claims no traditional status but only a human status ... This dissolution of society, as a particular class, is the *proletariat*.[9]

If the proletariat is the last historical class, it is because its coming to power in what Marx calls the 'dictatorship of the proletariat' is the prelude to the building of a society in which all will stand in the same relation to the means of production, as their collective owners. 'Worker' now no longer designates a particular class membership, but simply all men and women who contribute to producing and sustaining social life. This first phase of the anti-capitalist revolution is known to Marx as socialism, and it is not one which will involve complete equality. Indeed, Marx sees the whole notion of 'equal rights' as itself inherited from the bourgeois epoch, as a kind of spiritual reflection of the exchange of abstractly equal commodities. This is not to say that for him the concept lacks value, but that it inevitably represses the particularity of men and women, their uniquely different endowments. It thus acts among other things as a form of mystification, concealing the true content of social inequalities behind a mere legal form. In the end, Marx himself is concerned more with difference than with equality. Under socialism, it remains the case that

> ... one man is superior to another physically or mentally and so supplies more labour in the same time, or can labour for a longer time; and labour, to serve as a measure, must be defined by its duration or intensity, otherwise it ceases to be a standard of measurement. This *equal* right is an unequal right for unequal labour. It recognizes no class differences, because everyone is only a worker like everyone else; but it tacitly recognizes unequal privileges. *It is, therefore, a right of inequality, in its content, like every right.* Right by its very nature can consist only in the application of an equal standard; but unequal individuals (and they would not be individuals if they were not unequal) are measurable only by an equal standard in so far as they are brought under an equal point of view, are taken from one *definite* side only, for instance, in the present case, are regarded *only as workers* and nothing more is seen in them, everything else being ignored. Further, one worker is married, another not; one has more children than another, and so

on and so forth. Thus, with an equal performance of labour, and hence an equal share in the social consumption fund, one will in fact receive more than another, one will be richer than another, and so on. To avoid all these defects, right instead of being equal would have to be unequal. ('Critique of the Gotha Programme', SW 324)

Socialism, then, is not about some dead-levelling of individuals, but involves a respect for their specific differences, and allows these differences for the first time to come into their own. It is in this way that Marx resolves the paradox of the individual and the universal: for him, the latter term means not some supra-individual state of being, but simply the imperative that everyone should be in on the process of freely evolving their personal identities. But as long as men and women still need to be rewarded according to their labour, inequalities will inevitably persist.

The most developed stage of society, however, which Marx dubs communism, will develop the productive forces to a point of such abundance that neither equality nor inequality will be in question. Instead, men and women will simply draw from the common fund of resources whatever meets their needs:

In a higher phase of communist society, after the enslaving subordination of the individual to the division of labour, and therewith also the antithesis between mental and physical labour, has vanished; after labour has become not only a means of life but life's prime want; after the productive forces have also increased with the all-round development of the individual, and all the springs of cooperative wealth flow more abundantly – only then can the narrow horizon of bourgeois right be crossed in its entirety and society inscribe on its banners: 'From each according to his ability, to each according to his needs!' (Ibid. 325)

In communist society we would be free of the importunity of social class, and have the leisure and energy instead to cultivate our personalities in whatever way we chose, provided that this respected the injunction that everyone else should be allowed to do so too. What distinguishes this political goal most sharply from liberalism is the fact that, since for Marx an expression of our individual being is also a realization of our species-being, this process of exploring and evolving individual life would be carried out reciprocally, through mutual bonds, rather than in splendid isolation. The other is seen by Marx as the means to my own self-fulfilment, rather than as at best a mere co-entrepreneur in the project or at worst as an active obstacle to my own self-realization. Communist society would also turn the productive forces bequeathed to it by capitalism to the end of abolishing as far as possible all degrading labour, thus releasing men and women from the tyranny of toil and enabling them to engage in the democratic control of social life as 'united individuals' newly in charge of their own destinies. Under communism, men and women can recuperate their alienated powers and recognize the world they create as their own, purged of its spurious immutability.

But socialist revolution requires an agent, and this Marx

discovers in the proletariat. Why the proletariat? Not because they are spiritually superior to other classes, and not necessarily because they are the most downtrodden of social groups. As far as that goes, vagrants, outcasts, the destitute – what Marx rather witheringly calls the 'lumpen-proletariat' – would serve a good deal better. One might claim that it is capitalism itself, not socialism, which 'selects' the working class as the agent of revolutionary change. It is the class which stands to gain most by the abolition of capitalism, and which is sufficiently skilled, organized and centrally located to carry out that task. But the task of the working class is to carry out a specific revolution – that against capitalism; and it is thus in no sense necessarily in competition with other radical groups – say, feminists or nationalists or ethnic activists – who must carry through their own particular transformations, ideally in alliance with those most exploited by capitalism.

What form would this society take? Certainly not that of a state-run social order. The political state for Marx belongs to the regulatory 'superstructure' of society: it is itself a product of class struggle rather than sublimely beyond that conflict, or some ideal resolution of it. The state is ultimately an instrument of the governing class, a way of securing its hegemony over other classes; and the bourgeois state in particular grows out of an alienation between individual and universal life:

> … out of this very contradiction between the interest of the individual and that of the community the latter takes an independent form as the *State*, divorced from the real interests of individual and community, and at the same

time as an illusory communal life, always based, however, on the real ties existing in every family and tribal
conglomeration – such as flesh and blood, language,
division of labour on a larger scale, and other interests –
and especially, as we shall enlarge upon later, on the
classes, already determined by the division of labour,
which in every such mass of men separate out, and of
which one dominates all the others. It follows from this
that all struggles within the State, the struggle between
democracy, aristocracy, and monarchy, the struggle for
the franchise, etc. etc., are merely the illusory forms in
which the real struggle of the different classes are fought
out among one another. (GI 53)

Marx did not always take such a briskly instrumentalist
view of the state in his detailed analyses of class conflicts;
but he is convinced that its truth, so to speak, lies outside
itself, and sees it moreover as a form of alienation all in
itself. Each individual citizen has alienated to the state part
of his or her individual powers, which then assume a
determining force over the everyday social and economic
existence which Marx calls 'civil society'. Genuine socialist
democracy, by contrast, would rejoin these general and
individual parts of ourselves, by allowing us to participate
in general political processes as concretely particular individuals – in the workplace or local community, for example, rather than as the purely abstract citizens of liberal
representative democracy. Marx's final vision would thus
seem somewhat anarchistic: that of a cooperative common-
wealth made up of what he calls 'free associations' of
workers, who would extend democracy to the economic

sphere while making a reality of it in the political one. It was to this end – not one, after all, very sinister or alarming – that he dedicated, not simply his writings, but much of his active life.

NOTES

1. 'Theses on Feuerbach', in Lewis S. Feuer (ed.), *Marx and Engels: Basic Writings on Politics and Philosophy* (London, 1969), p. 286.

2. *Karl Marx: Early Writings* (Harmondsworth, 1975), p. 257. All quotations from this work are taken from Marx's *Economic and Philosophical Manuscripts* of 1844. Subsequent references to this work as EW are given in parentheses after quotations.

3. Feuer, p. 283.

4. Karl Marx, *The German Ideology*, edited and introduced by C.J. Arthur (London, 1974), p. 47. Subsequent references to this work as GI are given in parentheses after quotations.

5. 'The Communist Manifesto', in *Marx and Engels: Selected Works* (London, 1968), p. 38. Subsequent references to this work as SW are given in parentheses after quotations.

6. The second part of this quotation is taken from Karl Marx, *Capital*, Vol. 1 (New York, 1967), p. 178. Subsequent references to this work are given as C in parentheses after quotations.

7. Karl Marx, *Grundrisse* (Harmondsworth, 1973), p. 488.

8. Karl Marx, *The Holy Family* (London, 1956), p. 125.

9. Karl Marx, 'Contribution to the Critique of Hegel's Philosophy of Right', in T. Bottomore (ed.), *Karl Marx: Early Writings* (London, 1963), p. 58.